CW00798773

TOBACCO SMU
—TAX PAID

TOBACCO SMUGGLING
—TAX PAID

by

Paul McGoldrick

DIADEM BOOKS

Tobacco Smuggling – Tax Paid

All Rights Reserved. Copyright © 2010 Paul McGoldrick

No part of this book may be reproduced or transmitted in any form or by any means, graphic, electronic, or mechanical, including photocopying, recording, taping or by any information storage or retrieval system, without the permission in writing from the copyright holder.

The right of Paul McGoldrick to be identified as the author of this work has been asserted in accordance with the Copyright, Designs and Patents Act 1988 sections 77 and 78.

The views expressed in this work are solely those of the author and do not necessarily reflect the views of the publisher, and the publisher hereby disclaims any responsibility for them.

Published by Diadem Books
Distribution coordination by Spiderwize

For information, please contact:

Diadem Books
Mews Cottage
The Causeway
KENNOWAY
The Kingdom of Fife
KY8 5JU

www.diadembooks.com

ISBN:978-0-9559852-5-6

Dedication

To all bipolars who have gone before me—may they rest in peace.

Epigraph

To be sane or not to be sane—that is the question.

Foreword

Paul McGoldrick is a larger than life character with a heart of gold whose book reflects his personal journey through the ups and downs of life. Combine life's normal obstacles with a bipolar disorder where he is prone to "highs" and the adventures come thick and fast. This account is a frank, humorous, easy to read yet profound insight into one person's journey through life while dealing with a severe and enduring mental illness.

People with bipolar disorder experience episodes of extreme mood swings, which range from mania to depression. Bipolar disorder is thought to affect 1 in every 100 adults at some time during their life. It used to be called Manic Depression and in clinical practice it is sometimes called Bipolar Affective Disorder.

Bipolar Scotland is a registered Scottish charity (SC021705) whose vision is to enhance the quality of life of people with bipolar disorder and their carers, including friends and relatives, by offering appropriate support at both individual and group level.

We are delighted that Paul has chosen to support Bipolar Scotland with the proceeds from the book as we are reliant on donations and grants to fund the work we do.

This book is very easy to read, yet will give the reader an insight into this condition as experienced by Paul. The manifestation of bipolar disorder varies greatly from person to person.

Alison Cairns
Chief Executive
Bipolar Scotland

Chapter One

WELL, WHERE DO I BEGIN? Oh yeah! Nearly forgot. I was standing outside Levante Psychiatric Hospital, alias 'El Loony-Bino', near Benidorm on Spain's Costa Blanca, having just been liberated from another three weeks of voluntary head shrinking therapy for my ever-occurring manic episodes, only to be met by my two elderly, anguished parents. They had just arrived after coming all the way from Scotland to rescue me from my conceptions of medicated hospitality, this being one of the conditions of release, like a precaution to make sure I would be able to readjust after being administered with the meds that go with the illness.

I was an international manic-depressive. I had experienced previous episodes in Turkey, Tenerife, Spain, England, France and Ireland. Each one was better than the one before, but unfortunately they do not last and you have the mayhem of the downside, which brings you to a dark labyrinth of suicidal depression. That's the problem with my delirious lifestyle, you see—the highs are too high and the lows are too low—more ups 'n downs than the grand old duke himself. Thank heavens for lithium, a mood stabilising drug, tried and tested for nearly 60 years. It works for me! I had a lithium deficiency, you see, a lack of a vital natural salt in the body, that's all. Give the sufferer the lithium and more often than not he or she will be fine—just like a diabetic with an insulin deficiency. Sad to say, I wouldn't listen to the mental health professionals for years. I knew better, and oh boy, how wrong I was! But then, I left school in 1978 with no academic qualifications, so go figure!

As my parents approached, all seemed bright, rosy and wonderful, to say the least. After all, I hadn't seen them for three months. After heading for international territory at the drop of a hat with no consideration for anyone, I was still in the throes of a manic episode, but managed to convince the Spanish doctors I was ready for discharge. I might have been mad, but I wasn't stupid! I learned to speak Spanish in 1985 whilst living in Tenerife, after yet another episode, and the docs managed to be taken in with my Spanish blarney. Anyway, I was released into my 'Walter Mitty' world yet again, enjoyed a few days in Benidorm with mum 'n dad, and then, yes, you guessed it—more mayhem! Whilst I was in the nutcracker suite, my flat was broken into and my passport stolen. Who cares? I thought. I'll just stay in Spain forever, not giving a second's consideration for my aging parents.

My mother left no time to the imagination and suggested we get in touch with the British Consulate in Alicante, as we were due home the next day. Okay, says me, it's a glorious day and I'll take this opportunity of a nice drive to Alicante just to keep my parents happy. How considerate was that! Within five minutes, there she was, a clapped out 25-year-old transit van with broken windscreen, bald tyres and a roaring exhaust! These were the good bits. I had salvaged her from another failed property maintenance venture on the Costas, and luckily enough she was still running—just!

My parents looked at me as if I had four heads. "All aboard!" I shouted, and in they got, totally against their will, knowing that the consulate was my only chance of getting back to Scotland. They would have been more comfortable going three rounds with Tyson due to the rumbling and banging from the disrepair of the springs and shock absorbers. A right-hand drive deathtrap driving on the wrong side of the road with a manic chauffeur behind the wheel was not an ideal style of transportation. Along the way, all I could talk about was the mad drivers and the terrible condition of *their* vehicles. So there we were, *honk honk, screech screech*, as I was giving way to the right forgetting I was on the wrong side of the road in a country that drives on the right. We had to be at the consulate for 3 p.m. to allow for the necessary photos and form filling. It was 2.30 p.m. and we still had 60kms to go. Foot to the floor and we somehow made it, though not without minor problems en route—engine overheating, smoke billowing from radiator, etc.

All went well at the passport office and we headed on the return leg of the journey, which was just as crazy as the outward, only worse. As I looked in my cracked rear view mirror, I saw Spanish motorists swerving to and fro to avoid the calamity of the van's rear door, which was unexpectedly deposited in their path. I carried on regardless, thinking, "Well, at least I took my parents for a tour round the picturesque coast."

The next day we headed home to Scotland, me heavily medicated with sleepers. I have no recollection of the journey, immigration, baggage reclaim—nothing. I came to at my parents' home with two psychiatric nurses towering over me. Mum had phoned ahead as she knew my condition was far from stable. They suggested I go voluntarily to the laughing academy at Monklands Psychiatric Hospital, and with a little protest (as I was stating my case of extreme sanity), I finally granted their wishes. After all, I was going in to cure all those poor folk with mental health problems. I was okay, you see. I could become very benevolent, buy them cigarettes, teach them guitar and computer, and tell them they were okay, not to listen to the staff, and inform them the drugs don't work so what the hell!

I met a few people inside I knew very well, who shall remain nameless, of course. There were schizophrenics, bi-polars (the new name for manic depressives) like myself, voice hearers, split personality sufferers, the clinically depressed, all sorts of beautiful human beings with mental health problems through no fault of their own. But it was their lucky day—Paul McNuts had arrived!

"Lets party!" I said.

Out came the guitar and the place erupted. The poor nurses were telling us to keep the noise down in the dayroom—they had a thankless, monumental task with twenty-odd loon-tunes in one small room going full throttle with Dylan's 'Knocking on Heaven's Door'—never mind the fact that all twenty of us (not just one!) were flying recklessly over the cuckoo's nest right there in the modified concert hall.

As night fell, the local constabulary brought in yet another victim to the acute admissions unit. Well, thanks to what followed, I really think that might have been the last time those rookie policemen would want to offer their services for escorting patients to this sanctuary. The scene was set, and I gave the orders to my disturbed comrades to wait till the rookies were passing the windows of our dayroom on their way back to their van. "Go!" I shouted, and we all ran straight to the windows, banging and screaming like a demented tribe of savage psychopaths!

You never saw two young policemen hightail it so fast in all your existence! What a laugh! They dashed for their van like Olympic sprinters and were off like rats up a drainpipe. One-upmanship was ours to claim as our own. Meds were administered and the night became tranquillised, a sense of relief all around for the amused staff who informed us they actually enjoyed the fun of the night's wound-up events at the expense of P.C. Plod.

Morning broke to the sounds of "Nurse! Nurse! I've shat myself, I've shat myself!" My meds weren't agreeing with me and this in turn led to my first shit haemorrhage—evidence all over jammies, bed sheets, the works! It smelt like a skunk's vomit! Nurses rushed to help me deal with my aromatic disaster that dripped from the side of the bed. John, the staff nurse, slipped on the brown excrement as he raced to my rescue and went down like a whore's knickers only to get up unassisted by Wee Mary, the student nurse who was in a fit of convulsions with laughter. She was soon to change her mood when John called for reinforcements in the way of domestic staff and ordered her to give them a hand to clean the shite. I was christened "Shitey Arse" by the other patients and thought, "How can I get my own back on these numbskulls who had severely dented my pride?"

Yes, I had the solution! Just a bit of light-hearted fun, really. So I phoned my brother Liam and asked him to go to Tam Shepard's joke shop and get me thirty sachets of itching powder. No sooner had I asked and wallah! the consignment was delivered. I waited for evening meal time, excused myself and went about my revengeful duties, sprinkling beds at random, though intentionally not doing them all so as I wouldn't look guilty—which I would if I was the only bed that wasn't sabotaged! I waited patiently for my friends to retire to their beds and within two minutes the bedlam began—twelve beds full of what I can only describe as demented jumping beans, if you can imagine, legs, hands, feet, arses all twitching and shaking like synchronised epileptics looking for a cure.

We had a lot of fun in those sanctuaries full of beautiful people with problems.

Chapter Two

CONTRARY TO PUBLIC BELIEF I would rather spend time with my kind of folk than the normal people on the outside, whatever normal is. They tell me it's like a cycle on a washing machine, and most wouldn't harm a fly. As I'm sure you are aware, a load of stigma is attached to mental health. Let me illustrate. I am a manic-depressive, right? Before my diagnosis I thought the word *manic* stood for *maniac*—maybe just my ignorance, I don't know, but I believe, and its only my opinion, that they changed the name *manic depression* to *bi-polar* to help break down the stigma. It was a great relief to find out 'manic' simply means 'high'; therefore with bi-polar we have two poles, one positive+ and one negative-, just like the terminals (poles) on a car battery! We have all heard of Beatle mania, or Michael Jackson mania, right? It's the best way I can describe my affliction, and I must emphasise I'm not a mental health professional, which means I can only describe my condition in layman's terms as I have experienced and suffered it. Take a vein or artery in your head, for example; call it a pipe, a tube, whatever you may; now, we all have brain chemistry, dopamine, serotonin, endorphin, to name a few. Sometimes we get too much or too little running through these veins, making us too high or too low, giving us a sense of elation or depression. Lithium, a mood stabiliser, works for me, thank God!

Incidentally, I'm not religious. I think God is more than enough, whoever He, She or It may be. I wouldn't be arrogant enough to explain God, as it tells us in all the great religious books that it's beyond human understanding; but I do believe that deep down, every man and woman has a fundamental idea of God, just like the atheist that said, "Thank God I'm an atheist!" Today, I'm the happiest man I know, and I don't say that flippantly, but after travelling through 44 years of mental torture with my fair share of suicide attempts, I have come to realise it's an inside job—the blame game has got to stop. All my life I blamed people, places and things, and ironically looked for happiness in the same. But then I learned to depend on me! As it says in the song, 'the greatest love of all.' We all know we can't love anyone till we love ourselves, but I believe we can't love ourselves till we love everyone else. Call me what you may, you are entitled to your opinion, but I've learned in my experience that all people are the same, human beings with faults, so who am I to criticise?

I don't want to come across as some kind of saint—I don't want to be a saint (all the saints I know are dead), but what I do know is that I've got to this beautiful place today through a lot of pain, which I prefer to call growth. Therefore I'll never be in pain again, only growth. My recovery has been due to a few priceless assets, the love of my family, the mental health profession, forgiveness and acceptance…and in the acceptance lies the solution to all my life's problems. So profound! Not another silly cliché, but I had to build it from my head to my heart, and I managed this with a lot of growth and soul searching. I can only say that forgiveness is more for self than for the other party—a beautiful gift that can bring instant peace of mind, so why not try it?

Life's too short not to forgive. How did I reach the stage of forgiveness that I'm at now, you ask? It was by understanding that whatever people do at any given time, they only do due to lack of understanding of self; therefore they think it's the right thing to do… and before you jump down my throat, no, I don't condone injustices.

Having been blighted with superstition in my early life, this was one of the contributions to my ongoing instability. In my crazed head I blamed the number 13, amongst other insane ideas, as it was to follow me all my life, right to the present day. You see, I was born at 166f Dundyvan Road, Coatbridge, the 3 digits totalling, yes, 13! I then moved with my parents to number 13c; from there it was 131, 13 back to front *and* front to back! Next was number 13 itself, and now I live at number 139—yes, 3 digits totalling once again 13 with monotonous regularity. Today I just laugh at it and put it down to nothing more than coincidence. Makes for good conversation, all the same.

As a kid all my friends said I was mad. Sure, they meant it with the best possible intentions, meaning that I was good fun, good for a laugh, always playing the practical joker, two shades the right side of crazy! Just another indication of my desire to be liked, really.

As I developed into adolescence and my teens, I became an amateur boxer. I gave it up when I got fed up getting knocked out! I was so far behind in points in one of my bouts that I needed to knock out my opponent to get a draw.

My boxing skills were to take me down a road I'm not proud of today. The situation was that at the weekends all of my little gang would indulge in a tipple or three of "what the fuck are you looking at" juice—a potent potion notoriously cheap and commonly known as BUCKFAST TONIC WINE, which guaranteed more transformation than the elixir imbibed by Dr Jekyll and Mr Hyde. Ironically, this heady concoction was manufactured by the monks in Devon, in England! We would then proceed to go up the town to the dens of iniquity and start all sorts of territorial wars, fighting with anyone unfortunate enough to cross our path. All the lads from the other ghettos would be intoxicated to the same degree, a recipe for disaster.

I didn't drink in those days, you see. My troops would start the battle, of course, and since not one of them could beat a drum, I had to come to their rescue—jab jab, 1, 2, 1, 2, and before long you had three or four of the opposition lying spread-eagled, sparked out! It makes me shiver today as I hear all the stories in the news about people who have been killed with one blow! My ego kicked in big time and I couldn't wait till the next morning to get down the local pub, stick my chest out and bask in the applause of the crowd.

"Archie (my nick name), you're some fighter!"

"Thanks, thanks..."

This was another way to satisfy my need to be liked, as I see it today. All I was doing was taking advantage of some young lads who had too much of the booze and didn't have the ability to defend themselves. I was a liberty-taker but didn't know any better.

I was to go on to establish an ever-growing reputation of being even madder, as the town of Coatbridge gave me the name 'Mad Archie from Langloan'. At 19 or 20, I thought this was really positive for my survival. So there you have it! The difference between the tags of being 'funny mad' as a kid and 'really mad' as a young adult were not that clear to me, at first, so when I began to experience my voluntary admissions into loony-bins in 1997, I thought, "They'll be calling me Mad Archie and Big Mad McGoldrick now!" All right, I admit, this was exceedingly painful, not like Mr Kipling's good cakes—I had no self-esteem, no self worth, just a broken, torn, poor ego nearly stripped of dignity; but I hung in there with the skin of my teeth. All my life I had no self-esteem. I managed to build it up at least to 'low' (a car can run on a low level of oil, can't it?), and have managed to maintain that ever since.

So, to summarise, in my mind I was a total loser, no one liked me, a bully, a liberty- taker, a con man, and all things negative—sticks and stones will break my bones, but names will hurt me more. Apparently, the people who say they don't care what others think of them are the ones who suffer more. I can definitely go along with that, and I can tell you the pain was excruciating.

At St. Augustine's primary school in Coatbridge I was very bright, always first or second or thereabouts in all my subjects, but I always felt like a lost soul, never fitting in anywhere, like a square peg in a round hole, if the truth be told. But I could always disguise this with acting the fool, as I've already mentioned.

So, I had this desire to be popular. Maybe it's not surprising, therefore, that one of my endeavours was to become a thief at a very early age.

Chapter Three

TO BE A THIEF was certainly not my intention. Every Sunday night I would steal a half crown (12 pence) from my mother's purse. I would spend half on juice and chocolate, and give the other half to the 'African Babies Society'. I think this was to ease my conscience.

We used to call them "the black babies", but, apparently this a'int politically correct now. So do I call them the ethnic babies? And oh yeah, that reminds me—I'll have to get a tin of ethnic boot polish. The mind boggles.

This two-fold venture of mine, of thief and beneficiary, as I see it today, was for two reasons: (1) I was a thief (you can't be half pregnant), and (2) I wanted the pat on the back. You see, whoever gave the most to the black babies (as you did in those days) was brought up to the front of the class and given a big round of applause...a desire to be liked again, you see. I thought I was a modern-day Robin Hood, robbing the middle-class and giving to the poor. The kids in the class were probably thinking, "He's an arsehole, he's given more to the black babies than we get for a week's pocket money!"

I passed my 11-plus with distinction and moved on to Columba High (August '74). Now, I've heard that bi-polar (manic depression) can manifest in early adolescence. Well, I can certainly vouch for that. Happy, mad, glad and sad, all in five minutes, up and down like a whore's knickers! At Columba I was still managing to stay toppish of the class for my first year, and left with zilch, nothing, nante, blank—yes, the centre of a doughnut. With the benefit of hindsight I put this down to three attributes: (1) A serious head knock (I'm laughing when I hear you say 'absolutely!'); (2) the illness, and (3) the fact that money became my god. Whatever the three were to blame, my education went out the window.

When I was 14 my friends and I would go to the YMCA on a Monday night for a youth club and we would engage in many different activities. On this particular evening our youth leader came up with the crazy idea that we run blindfold up and down the concrete-built sports hall, the object being that some would be blindfolded and told to race the length of the hall with our un-blindfolded friends acting as our guide dogs, shouting "Go, Stop, Turn", etc. I had really good friends in those days, you see—they told me to keep running. Just imagine a 9-stone 14-year-old boy, swift as a deer, running blindfold all out until he SMASHES, yes, full tilt into a concrete wall nose first! I ended up with a face like a melted basin. Seriously, I reckon I was lucky to survive what happened. The concerned face of the nurse is all I remember. I had severe concussion and was admitted to Monklands Hospital for ten days. My concentration has never been the same since... What was I saying? Oh yes, concentration... Well, you've got to laugh.

I then got into the mode of thinking a crate of milk bottles was a cow's nest. I was definitely a French fry short of a Happy Meal! My short-term memory was shot to bits. At school I began to dodge lessons more and more and decided to start my own empire, thinking education could go and fuck itself. I was stupid anyway, I thought. I would go to Collin's jewellery auctions in Glasgow with my mother, telling her we had a half day holiday from school for whatever reason. Then I would buy one or two watches very cheaply, maybe a pair of earrings and a shitey wee bracelet, all for pennies, I might add. I would double my money, I reasoned—plus more, quite likely, at my newly formed trade centre at the back of the smokers' huts at school. This was my shout: "NO FANCY SHOPS! NO FANCY PRICES! NO ESCALATORS OR ELEVATORS! WE'RE ON THE GROUND FLOOR. HURRY! HURRY MRS MURRAY! THE WHOLE JOLLY LOT HAS TO GO!" Occasionally I would add, "HURRY BEFORE THE POLICE COME, IT'S ALL STOLEN," knowing that the people I knew anyways would be more keen to buy if it were stolen.

This trick was to follow me throughout my life and, sad to say, got me the reputation of being a thief or a con man, or both. Nobody's fault but my own, of course. But there were a lot of jealous people out there trying to slander me even more. My conscience is clear today and thankfully I have no criminal convictions. There would be 30 or 40 mad screaming kids fighting for the crown jewels! Remember, I only had a few items, so I saw a niche in the market. As fast as you could say ABC, I was straight back into the auctions.

I did become a wee thief. We had a teacher, Mr McAuthor—'Mad George', he was known as (see, I stigmatised in those days as well). He would take a count for the weekly dinner tickets and mark the numbers on the sheet. He would then send me, 'cos I was his mate. I always had this ability of telling people what they wanted to hear, better known as BULLSHIT. So down to the principal's office I would go to collect these tickets. Mad, you see? But not stupid! I would erase the numbers and write in a few more for myself. I'm not proud of this today, but this gave me the ability to increase my stock and variety at my newly formed trade centre. (Richard Branson, eat your heart out!) I don't want to be a billionaire; I just want to be happy. By this time I could earn £20 a day—not a bad wage for a kid back in the mid-70s. At this time I also had an aunty who lived in Cherbourg, France. She would bring me all sorts of miniature perfumes and yes, tobacco as well. There was no duty paid on this merchandise, but who cared? There was a market for it at my school shop. I must have been the youngest bakky smuggler in history, with the unwitting assistance of old Aunt Sally, of course, my blood related accomplice.

As the years went on, my psychological duty of life was certainly paid. There came a chapter in my life when, I would say back in the 90s, I had a substantial wealth. Don't need or want it today. Looking back, the situation was that, when I was at my best financially, I was at my worst psychologically. Yes Gran, God rest you, you were right, it didn't bring me happiness. If only I had listened, but I reckon we have all to go down our own path.

Today I'm in heaven at last, and I'm staying here, 'coz in my opinion, it's a state of mind—yes, between your two ears. I can hear all you people who are so heavenly good you're no earthly use (you know who you are!) say, "Blasphemer!" (Giggle, giggle.) I also believe hell to be the same—a state of mind. That's the path I went down for 44 years, with suicidal tendencies on a very regular basis. Thank God, once again, for my family, lithium, acceptance and forgiveness. I'm 47 today and have been free of my suffering for three years, every day better than the next. I would go down that road again to get to this beautiful place, but I also have the added advantage to know that life is not a destination, it's a beautiful journey, and for all this, all I have to do is take two tiny little pills every day. "What a deal!" as I would say in my old trading days.

Testimony to my Gran again. "Paul," she said, "nothing on the outside can be dirty, it's only what comes from the inside that can be dirty!" Apart from negative thinking, gossip can be the next biggest killer on earth. I know, 'coz I was one. It kills the spirit and can also kill the physical.

Chapter Four

IN THE SUMMER OF '97 I vividly remember my first acute manic episode. It led me to Stratheden Psychiatric Hospital in Cupar, in Fife, Scotland.

An idea took flight in my mind that I was going to be a property maintenance tycoon very soon. I invested in a 30-year old £200 clapped-out caravan, and wondered why my girlfriend at the time, Patricia, wouldn't go to the caravan park with me. Flaking paint, tatties growing in the interior, broken windows, almost tartan in colour, something you wouldn't be seen dead in, and all I could think of was me and my millionaire status, so off I went. I set sail for the east, having hooked her up to what I can only describe as an old Jeep of the same condemned condition. Anstruther holiday camp, here I come!

My fledgling business plan was to take a monumental blow. I only got three miles up the road when I smelt something burning. The electrics on the tow bar were like a towering inferno, so I proceeded to do the manly thing. I pulled over to extinguish the unexpected flames, but where was I to find the water? Well, a man's got to do what a man's got to do, so out it came with urine to the rescue. Red Adair would have been proud of me. Piss, piss, piss, job done! I burnt my hand unhooking the caravan and haven't seen it (the caravan, not my hand) since, leaving it smouldering in a layby in Cumbernauld.

But no matter—everything was wonderful. I was as high as Ryanair, Easyjet and Brittish Airways all rolled into one. Taking into account I hadn't slept for four days, I was driving like a bat out of hell, desperate to get to my business destiny in the old boneshaker. You see, I was going to start my property maintenance scheme by buying Anstruther Holiday Park, a place where I had limited fond memories as a child. I arrived at two in the morning, thinking I would celebrate with a wee tipple before I become the new Bill Gates, sleep being the last thing on my mind. I wanted to party, so off I went on my rounds, rattling caravan windows 'n doors, asking if anyone was up for a knees up. I could crawl up and die if I imagine what the poor souls were thinking—"Who's this loony waking us from a good night's sleep on our vacation in the middle of the night!" But I persisted and got my just rewards.

Whose door should I have banged on but an old alkie friend from the Brig, Big Jim, the Brig being Coatbridge! Is it true that every village has an idiot? Well, they say there's five in every house in the Brig. They were going to change the name to Bethlehem, but couldn't find three wise men and a virgin—what a town! Anyway Big Jim had plenty of ammo—wine, beer 'n scotch, it was my lucky night! We bullshitted till dawn whilst making a heavy dent in the ammo. He crashed to sleep and I stole the remainder of what was left of John Barleycorn, Mr Booze, and proceeded to talk pish to the animals in the adjoining field. Time was getting on and I thought to myself, what's my next plan of action? I know, let's secure accommodation!

I was homeless 'n destitute, it occurred to me, and I didn't want to stay in Jim's van where the rats inside were running around in boiler suits. The place smelt like a kipper's arse! But my elated state informed me all was rosy, and at 9.02 a.m. I approached the site office notwithstanding my somewhat intoxicated state. I looked at the caravan sales board, found a 19-year-old 8-berth caravan that looked very modern for the year and said to the receptionist, "I'll take this one!"

Two grand just like that! My hand dipped into my shabby trouser pocket and poured the money onto the sales desk.

"Don't you want to view before you buy, sir?" said the receptionist.

"No," said I, "I'm a gypsy, I know a good deal when I see one thanks, and there's a hundred for yourself!"

Being very irresponsible with money is another symptom of the illness. The girl had a look of severe shock on her pretty little face. She gave me a key, asked me if I wanted a receipt, which I declined, and headed for my new residence, number H24. I was made!

I decided to have my house warming all alone. Illusions of grandeur were installed and I was going to buy the full caravan site, on a rent-to-buy deal, then thought I may as well have a wee drink to celebrate, went to the local off sales and spent £300 on a carry-out—bottles of whisky, vodka, a case of buckie, beer lager, the works! By the time I got back to the site all the kids were playing outside. I attracted their attention by shouting, "Who wants money?!" and began to throw crisp £20 notes about. They swarmed like flies round shite! They must have thought Christmas had come early. I dread to wonder what their parents were thinking if they were informed.

When I got back to my new found residence there they were—Tonto and the Lone Ranger! They had been on my trail since I left the Brig. The good Samaritans had arrived to help salvage any shreds of sanity I might have left—yes, my mum and Patricia. My mum informed me the doctor was on the way. I went ballistic and smashed up my new home!

This was the first and only time I was violent during my manic episodes, and I *was* violent! After all, it was my home to smash. I could imagine the men with the white coats coming down the caravan park with the straightjackets. Without doubt, this would have seriously cramped my entrepreneurial style. I was a potential property millionaire, remember? A few minutes passed and sure enough, in came the doctor! He must have thought he was in Helmand Province, what with broken table legs, broken glass, ripped cushions, the contents of tomato ketchup bottles scattered down the walls and ceilings, fragments of ornaments everywhere—and this loony trying to plead his sanity. "There's fuck all wrong with me, mate!" I screamed. I didn't even have the courtesy to give the poor man his title. What an illness! Who the fuck gave my mother the right to phone the shrink? There was fuck-all wrong with me!

The doc was so nice, calm and understanding. No wonder—the shite was probably running down the crack in his arse!

"Paul," he said, "you'll be fine, just take this little tablet."

"*You* take it!" I said in my most sarcastic tone.

"Listen, Paul," he said, trying to sound reasonable, "your mother's an old woman, and she's very concerned."

"Concerned about *what!*" I exclaimed. "It's *my* house and I'll smash it if I so desire! Now fuck off! I'm not going out here in no straight jacket!"

"Paul, Paul, I'm here alone," he said reasonably, "but I suggest you go to the local hospital for a short assessment."

Watching his words carefully, he was, and not saying "Psychiatric Hospital"!

"What will they do there?" I asked. "Give me a new head, I suppose!"

He was very calming, and said I would be there in a voluntary capacity. After 15 minutes or so of deliberations, I took him up on his suggestions. I could imagine the sounds of *ME MAW, ME MAW ME MAW ME MAW* screaming from the ambulance coming down the caravan site, but this wasn't the case. Things were done very discretely, and the doctor took us all in his car.

Chapter Five

I WAS NEVER to see my new £2000 ABODE AGAIN! It's an expensive illness, this. The main reason in my head at the time for allowing the doctor to convince me to voluntarily go to the loony-bin was that recently I had someone very close to me that had had an admission and she could not handle what people were gossiping about her, and therefore tried to take her own life. Thank God she has the most beautiful life you could imagine today. God is good.

When I went in I thought, well, maybe this will help her, knowing that she wasn't the only one who had been in the nutcracker suite. But I can assure you, especially for you who know me, that my admission was necessary. I was as mad as a bag of spanners. I wouldn't harm a fly, except to say I once had to defend myself from a girl I went on holiday with in 2005. She had not taken her meds and became very psychotic, so there you have it—two loonies unmedicated together. I didn't know she was supposed to be on meds, but I wish her all the best today wherever she is.

I didn't lift my hand, I just sat on her. I'm twenty stone, and she was well less than half my weight. *SQUCHELCH*.

In most of my episodes I initially become the life 'n soul, an arsehole who has got to be the big spender. I don't sleep for maybe six days, I have a flight of ideas, I become delusional, I go to all sorts of European destinations at the drop of a hat, I streak, I think I'm Spiderman, AND hang from buildings, PLUS about another 1,000,000 things which are out of character when stable and on the level. And, as I said before, all I have to do is take two little tablets daily to prevent me from engaging in these sometimes-deadly pursuits.

Anyway, we approached the long winding drive, to Stratheden Loony-Bin's acute admissions ward. By this time I had settled down. After all, I was going in to prove a point to my friend, that others can go in too. So there I went, voluntarily, not realising I could get out voluntarily. What a con, I thought. Bastards! I wasn't sectioned, so I thought, what's the big deal? It sounded contradictory to me, but later I found out because I was high they kept me in for my own safety. I'll be eternally grateful to the staff.

In there I had my first experience with a beautiful self-harming girl called Angela, and she explained to me that if she was suffering emotional pain, she would cut herself with a blade to realise the pain, the physical pain counteracting the emotional pain. That's the only way she could describe it. She was sexually abused as a kid. She showed me her arms, and the only way I can describe the way they looked is to ask you to imagine thousands of tight elastic bands running up and down the length of your forearms, to make it look like very rough skin similar to the texture of an elephant's skin.

I was informed by my psychiatrist, Mr White, that I was in the throes of a manic episode. The only throes I knew about were the ones you got at wrestling, or the one my granny used to have on her bed.

"Well, Mr White," I said, "don't take whatever these 'throws' are away from me, 'coz I feel wonderful!"

If you can imagine the best feeling you have ever had, and multiply it by a zillion, well, that's only half as good as the feeling you get, and with me this 'throw' could last for up to six months! Given the choice to be manic, knowing that lithium was there as a back-up, would I have chosen to be bi-polar? Absolutely yes! My mind has taken me to some of the most beautiful destinations you earthlings will never be so fortunate to experience, Nirvana and more, and that's without a drink or a drug! Only us bi-polar bears have been lucky enough to take these feelings to our graves; and hopefully there will still be such moments, a moment at a time, though perhaps not an awful lot of them, when I will know that there is life before death.

But for every high there is a low.

I had one of the best times of my life in Stratheden and was liberated two weeks later, right back into the big bad world. But, I thought, if I binned the meds I would stay high—that would do for me, so into the bushes they went! I often wonder if those bushes were manic, blooming nuisances before I administered them meds—ha ha! I knew it all! I thought everyone was just jealous of my new-found happiness.

As Christmas approached I became suicidally depressed. The bushes had taken my meds, you see.

I would say I wouldn't wish it on my worst enemy, but I don't have any enemies today, therefore I wouldn't wish it on anyone today. To all you beautiful people with mental health problems, please, please take your meds! Surely I, and loonies like me who are taking the meds, are proof of this good advice. I didn't listen for 44 years, and feel very lucky that I'm here to tell the tale. I have the bonus of looking back whenever I want if I'm down, *naturally* down, I mean, and this soon lifts my spirits.

Today I adopt an attitude of gratitude, another one of my Gran's sayings. She had many sayings, and I've been lucky because I was able to transfer them from my head to my heart, because if you don't they are just clichés. If I can't be grateful for what I've got, I try to be grateful for what I've not got. I have a life second to none today.

Chapter Six

IN JANUARY '98 I joined Alcoholics Anonymous. Once again I was a binge drinker, three or four times a day, and I don't mean summer, winter, autumn and spring! You could say I was self-medicating my depressions! I found out in AA it's not so much what we drink as how often we drink that does the damage. It's what it does to us, and by God what it did to me! I was allergic to booze, you see. It brought me out in spots—spots like Aberdeen, London, Tenerife, Spain, police cells, courts—the list goes on and on.

I found out I was suffering from another illness, and that it was threefold—mental, physical and spiritual. It's the fist drink that gets you drunk. One is too many and a hundred isn't enough. When we take one it sets up what we alkies describe as the phenomenon of craving. I said to my mother one day, "Mum, my head's up my arse!" She said, "The next time your head's up your arse, have a look at your liver, Paul." I had an unmanageable life—alcoholism on top of suicidal depression. Financially I was sound, but I was a spiritual bankrupt.

AA is full of all kinds, as I'm sure some of you are aware—waitresses, lawyers, doctors, building workers, actors, cleaners, M.P.'s, rock stars—the full spectrum of humanity. We had a 12-step programme of recovery, which became so successful it is now been suggested as a programme of life by all the top religions in the world; on top of their own preaching, they say it has many analogies, one being it's like a big chocolate cake: if you eat it all at once you will be sick, but take it in baby portions and move on when you're ready, then take what's good for you and leave the rest behind, and you'll be well on your way to recovery.

The AA is full of sick people, none more so than myself. When I went—my first meeting was in 1988—I didn't stay, unfortunately. But it wasn't meant to be a one-day miracle cure. I've been sober for eight years now, but there is never a moment in time when I can say I won't drink again; but I certainly don't *want* to drink again. When I mention 'sick' people I don't mean 'bad' people—just sick people trying to get better a moment at a time. The medicine for the illness is the meetings of AA. I've been fortunate enough to have attended meetings all over the world—variety is the spice of life, they say! A lot of AA's tend to stick either by themselves, or in their own wee groups. I can't say whether this works for them, but I've had loads of suggestions in AA meetings—there are no musts, and the best one I have had is to separate the people from the programme.

I've had a few raw deals in the fellowship (you know who you are!) and given a few also. I have a beautiful, priceless programme in my life today, and no human being is powerful enough to take it from me. The few raw deals that I gave were mania-induced, but this ain't an excuse! We say in the fellowship there are a million excuses but not one reason! I believe this to be true, and I'm sorry, people, I wish you all the best with your future lives. KEEP COMING BACK!

Chapter Seven

BACK IN 1981 during the Maze Prison hunger strike in Northern Ireland, ten men died, and I was involved in a drunken fiasco. You see, I was never a bigot, but wanting to be liked, and this coupled up with peer pressure, I joined the local COATBRIDGE REPUBLICAN FLUTE BAND. Couldn't play a note, by the way, but was good on the comb and paper, mind you, though it meant the house was full of dandruff.

We frequently went to Andersontown in Belfast for republican marches. Now in those days there were a few guys in our little ghetto known as little Ireland who sold the *An-Phlobacht*, Gaelic for the *Republican News*. On the day Bobby Sands died our little ghetto flared up, nothing too spectacular, just some young lads like myself running about with banners that said 'Bobby Sands MP RIP'. I learned this with hindsight, as I was home in bed in a drunken stupor. This was about the time I finished boxing and started drinking.

Now the events that follow would make a TV drama or even movie. The Special Branch were installed in the nooks and crannies of our little ghetto, Langloan. The reason I know this was because I got roped in and was arrested, later to be charged with the prevention of terrorism act. The story goes that I had indulged in a couple of bottles of the bionic tonic earlier on in that day, and due to my severely intoxicated state, I was summoned by my troops (friends) to take an early bath. I poured myself a bath, fair enough, when I got home, but mother (bless her) hit me with rolling pin on route to my boudoir. Perhaps not surprisingly, I went into the land of drunken nods for a few hours. That's when I had the most vivid dream, that Langloan was up in arms. Walter Mitty again, I thought, but this particular dream, as it unfolded, proved to be as true as the ink on this page! I awoke to the screams of "Up the Provos! Yah British bastards, Brits out! Bobby Sands, Bobby Sands MP, MP!"

I thought, fuck this, I'm only interested in more alcohol, as us alkies were. I found out in AA that the onset of alcoholism can have a very quick onset! (In other words, it can happen very fast!) I proceeded to the front door clothed in slippers, sister's trousers (don't mean jeans), and my mother's jumper which fitted like a dog's coat on a hippo. Drat! The door was locked—this was mother's way of protecting her son from indulging in more alcohol, apart from hiding clothes, hiding keys, locking doors, etc… but us alkies are masters of being smart, or so we thought—in reality we were cheats, liars 'n thieves.

My mother's house in Kirkwood Street had a parapet under my bedroom window, so off I went out the window and down the pole supporting the parapet like Fireman Sam. Very little will prevent the thirsting alkie from getting his fix, you see.

Me maw, me maw, me maw! came the shrill screams of the emergency services siren, at the junction with Bank Street at the top of the street where my mother's residence was. Personally I didn't give a monkey's bollocks. I knew it would be something to do with Bobby's death, as I had earlier heard the chants. All I wanted was more alcohol, and in true commando style, I set off on my expedition to the Viking Night Club further up Bank Street.

In my fuzzy head I plotted the terrain that I was to cross, starting with my back yard. I went, like a troop on the run, jumping fences like they weren't there, through Kris Hanlons Close[1], using it like an observation post as I could see the police were out in numbers. I was taking no chances. I had to wait in my observation point for ten arduous minutes till the coast was clear!

The time was getting on, so I waggled like a time bomb ready to explode, as I needed my fix and the Viking shut at 2 a.m.! I didn't know what time it was—I just knew it was dark o' clock—oh Jesus, I thought, it might be closed already! But I wasn't going home to face wee Anna, my mum! She would fight the devil himself, and had a tongue to go along with it when the mood took her.

---

[1] Chris O'Hanlon Close?

Crouching all the way, hiding behind cars as I went, I managed to get as far as the back of the West End Hotel via Langloan Crescent, Langloan Place and Anderson steelworks lane Special Branch.

"Put your hands above your head and lie on the floor!" was the shout in a broad Northern Ireland accent.

I thought, for fuck's sake, get a grip! You see, nothing really frightens an alkie.

"Fuck off!" I said as I turned round and saw the pistol pointing between my two eyes. I still wasn't frightened as the alkie doesn't usually care whether he or she dies or not, as long as he or she gets a drink! By this time I was slowly but surely going into the throws of withdrawal.

"Wit is it?" I said.

"On the floor!" he screamed.

"Fuck off!" I said again. "I'll stick that pee-shooter up your arse!"

He cocked the pistol. I thought, this is a joke and, maybe luckily for me, his two accomplices came running, guns at the ready, screaming again: "On the floor ya bastard!" Everything was really blown out of proportion because of the recent unease in Ireland, and for all these police officers might have known, I could have been armed. I suppose they had a point.

Eventually I lay on the ground, thinking my mum and sister will kill me for getting their clothes dirty, as it was a gloomy rainy night even though we were in the month of May. No sooner had the meat wagon arrived when I was thrown into it, only to be confronted by wee Wullie O'Reilly, a fellow bevy merchant like myself, an 'any booze' wee man. I had more chance of getting a fright of a ghost! I was rattling! The DT's were waiting scarily around the corner, and Houdini himself couldn't have got out of this lions cage of a van, even if he were given oxy-acetylene burning gear. Here we go again! *Me maw me maw me maw me maw* in my ears. In my most sarcastic manner I managed to shout to the three Special Branch in the front: "Any swally?" (Well, I *thought* they were Special Branch—that's what they said, wasn't it?)

"Wit the fuk's happenin' Wullie?" I asked, turning to my companion in affliction.

"They lifted me for paintin' Bobby Sands on that wall at Andersons," he explained. "A coudnae even spell Bobby Sands."

Wullie was very clever but his craic[2] was magic.

---

[2] Craic or crack is a term for fun, entertainment, and enjoyable conversation.

"Is that aw, fuk sake! They got this wan wrang, huv they no! Fukin' pricks, wit aboot the Cowboy 'n Indians carry on! Did you see that fukin' edjit wi' the Tommie gun—thought he wiz John Wayne!"

Screech! We had arrived at Wittington cop shop, me 'n Wullie in our dulcet tones chanting "The boys of the old brigade", using the roof and the side walls of the van as our big base drum. To give the police credit, they didn't lay a finger on us. I would have kicked seven different shades of shite out of us!

"Wullie, how the fuk am a goin' to get a swally here in Alcatraz?"

"Wi' difficulty," he mused.

"Do you want to make a run for it?" says I.

"A run fur wit? We're in an 8 x 8 cell, ya dumpling!"

It was a reasonable suggestion, I thought. After all, I'd tried to run through a concrete wall before (going back to my days at the YMCA).

"Wit the fuk you talkin' aboot, McGoldrick!" he said again.

"Let me tell you, Wully, at school in '74…"

"Fuk, you 'n school!" Wullie interrupted as I was about to bore him with the YMCA story. "Wit aboot *this*?"

"Wit?" I said.

"This *here*, now, the tin pail, the jail, the cow's tail, call it wit you want," he said, "we're in the shit!"

"Wit fur? We'll be oot in ten minutes an I'll git tae the Viking fur a swally…"

"Oh really, is it open late this morning? It's 10 past three, ya fukin' bone heed!"

"Yir jokin' man!"

"If a wiz jokin' I wid have said!"

"Have ya heerd the one aboot the Viking shutting at 10 past 3, ya fukin' dikhead!"

"Here here, William—your language is choice this merry morning," I said in my best Etonian. But coming back to reality, I said, "Wit we gony do, Wullie?"

"Git a lawyer," he said.

"Naw, not that, Wullie, wit we gony do aboot a swally?" I said, coming back to the pressing matter in hand. "Then again," I continued. on reflection, "if I knew they corrupt

22

layers they might get us a swally." Always the optimist, I added, "But we'll be oot in ten minutes, Wullie…"

"Listen you," he said, "away 'n stick yir arse oot the windy, and go roon the back 'n throw stones at it, gie me piece tae think!"

"Tae think wit, Wullie?"

As I started to sing Billy Joel's "An Innocent Man" at the top of my voice (don't know how I was singing—I was rattling like a Donegal motorbike), in came the cavalry: two young smartly dressed gentlemen who introduced themselves as Special Branch.

"Wit's that?" I asked, "a tree that means a lot to somebody? A plant with special needs?"

They were not amused, and ran this spiel by us. Have you ever heard as much shite in all your existence? They accused us of being part of the Third Battalion IRA! To give them their due, however, they did not formally accuse us of this fanciful connection, though I have to say *I* was not amused by their flight of fancy.

"Away an throw shite at the moon!" I exclaimed. "Are you on drugs?" I said, and followed my question with another, more pertinent one: "If you are, can I get some?" Alcohol is a drug, you see, but that's another story.

"Cheeky bastard, McGoldrick," was the response I got.

"Aye," I rejoined, "but I can fight without guns, ya fukin' pansy boy." Becoming more reasonable, I continued, "Tell you what, get me a drink, and I'll confess to being the incarnation of James Connolly, and because I've a split personality condition, I'll be Kevi 'n Barry 'n James Joyce as well."

At that point I would have booted my balls, but again no violence was inflicted. I felt I had established a one-upmanship and verbally went on to character assassinate them to the bone. (I apologise for this today, retrospectfully, officers—but the delirium tremors were looming, see?)

I had to surrender, of course. I was incarcerated 'n trapped, like a rat in a cage. At that point I would have confessed to the Moors Murders for a swally! Alcohol is cunning, baffling 'n powerful. At that point I maintained my right to remain silent and said nothing, even though I hadn't been charged. The remainder of that morning was hell, with all the interrogation that followed and all without a fix!

We were finally charged under the prevention of terrorism act. Our lawyers appeared the next morning and all was revealed, due to the republican activity in Coatbridge, especially in Langloan. The police were taking no chances: they were acting on balderdash information that me and a few others were members of the IRA! The case went to court, but

I and a few "accomplices" were given a 'not proven' verdict. All the evidence they had was that Wullie, being a plater, had a small metal marking pen on him; and since I was an apprentice painter and decorator with the Monklands District Council, I had the means—wait for it!—of supplying the paint and painting the walls! Not guilty m'lud! It would have taken 10,000,000 of Wullie's pens to have scribbled Bobby Sands on the wall, as the figures were 6 feet high and 4 inches wide! Rolf Harris would have been proud of this work of art, and Wullie's pen was black, whereas the painting was in a creamy beige, better known as magnolia—a feat David Copperfield couldn't have mastered.

The story hit the national and international news headlines! During the case the judge temporarily closed and adjourned the court and ordered everyone—the accused, the defence and the prosecution—to go to the locus. We were conveyed under a police escort to Andersons wall, the scene of the crime! What a waste of the taxpayers' money! During the media leak our names and addresses were revealed. Can you imagine the mayhem! Our phones were jumping out of their sockets! Many of the lads who were of a UDA persuasion got our phone numbers from the telecommunications services and inundated families with the unsettling news they were going to be shot etc... Thankfully today I have more Protestant friends than Catholic, and can now freely go back and forth to my caravan in Garrison, Co. Fermanagh, where there's a beautiful mixed community.

Chapter Eight

SAD TO SAY I didn't give a shit about the threats arising from that IRA-UDA fiasco, but shiver to think of the stress I brought to my loving family. Yes, that was just one of the many dangerous situations the booze got me into! I'll reveal later how I had a gun put to my head yet again, by the Kurdish mafia whilst on a manic episode without alcohol, when I lived in Istanbul in 2000. And yes, I laughed and told them to fuck off again, and went back the next day to see if they wanted to carry on their proceedings. In mania you are not necessarily looking for trouble—more often than not you are simply fearless!

One story sticks in mind in particular. This time I became delusionally paranoid and thought the IRA and UDA were out to assassinate me—delusions of paranoia being one of the many side effects of bi-polar affective disorder. I joined the AA again, as I said, in January '98. Now, I don't mind breaking my anonymity, but I wouldn't break anyone else's. After all, if someone is meant to be anonymous, he or she must remain anonymous, one of our mottos being: who or what we see here, when we leave here, let it stay here!

So off I went to Ireland on an episode in October '98, an episode that ended in yet another admission to a psychiatric hospital (St. Columbus) in Co. Sligo, in the Free State of Ireland, just next to where Lord Mountbatten was blown up on his boat. My intentions were to start the first leg of my world tour in Ireland, and to personally say goodbye to my sister who lived on the border town of Garrison. I had just left my girlfriend of 12 years, Patricia, a diamond as I see her today, and set sail by catching a lift off a Derry car dealer who had been on business at Glasgow car auctions, to buy cars to resell in Ireland. It suited both of us that I drive a car over for him. He gets his car delivered and I get a free lift, and everyone's happy.

Now it was on the ferry that the conversation got to the Troubles. Conor the car dealer, and his best friend Malcolm, one Catholic and one Protestant, were heavily debating the current situation in Stormont, the Northern Irish parliament. I thought I had a little knowledge of Irish history, but by Jove, were these two young bucks well learned! It all started with laughter, but became quite heated. Nevertheless they shook hands and cuddled when their debate was concluded, the Catholic signing the sash and the protestant singing "The Wild Colonial Boy", not giving a hoot about all the other mixture of passengers. So in my head I thought these were brave or crazy men—they must be really connected to sing these patriotic songs in such a volatile location! Why were these other passengers not concerned? I mean, there was alcohol everywhere! You can imagine the situation. Funnily enough, lifting a drink was the last thing on my mind.

It so happened there was a Christian convention in Glasgow that weekend, and the ferry was jam-packed with Christians of both denominations; but I didn't find this out till years later when I asked Malcolm. He and Conor both knew this and knew they would get away with it.

We docked at Larne, and Malcolm proceeded to drive me to Co. Fermanagh as agreed. He was driving like Evil Kinevil, on roads that had more craters than the moon. All he spoke about was the paramilitaries, the IRA and the UDA, about smuggling ammo and guns over the border, etc. I might have been manic, but what was I to think? Yes, I surmised, the car boot was full of military apparatus! And then the penny really dropped!

Oh shit! He had just come from Glasgow, in a car that wasn't registered in his own name, and could freely sing sectarian songs on the boat, and was heading for the border— and I had a 'not proven' looming over my head even though a lot of years had passed since that earlier fiasco! *Get me the fuck out of here!* I thought, the paranoia kicking in big time!

We got to Garrison without incident. Betty was glad to see me but knew I was far from compos mentis. Wasting no time to say hello, I said, "Where's my jeep?" I had left it at Betty's two years earlier. "It's out the back yard," she said, "we've been using it today—it still drives," she said.

I was desperate to get to a meeting, and knew there was one in Bundoran, *a couple of miles across the border* in Co. Donegal! This is when the mega-delusional paranoia took off. You see, I knew there was a meeting as some AA's had told me, but I was approaching people on the streets and in shops saying things like "I'm a member of a fellowship and I'm looking for Jimmy the butcher or Sonny the barber" etc. See, most of us have an alias in the fellowship of alcoholics to protect anonymity. I didn't want to say AA, and certainly not the word 'anonymous', as only having been in AA a few months I thought this was breaking anonymity! What a fool I was—ha ha! Therefore I said 'fellowship'! Now, it has been known for the UDA and the IRA to be known as 'fellowships', so make your own conclusions! So referring to 'butcher' and 'barber'—well, what were the people to think? Sweeney Todd, with overtones of vicious butchers who committed atrocities down the ages... well, no wonder most of them put their heads down and got off their mark, or looked at me as if I had just got off a spaceship! You see, whatever persuasion these people were, they probably thought I was of the other persuasion, and that I wanted to kill, or maim Jimmy the Butcher or Sonny the Barber!

That's what my paranoia was starting to tell me after about a hundred people ignored me. I think most people would have been paranoid if they had realised the situation with hindsight. I eventually jumped in my jeep and headed to anywhere, just to get away from the paranoia. But I couldn't get rid off it. It came on me more and more like a psychological rash. I was looking in my rear view mirror and every car I saw behind me was the Provos, and every car approaching was the UDA, and I mean *every* car!

Night had fallen, and every person I was passing was a paramilitary out to kill this infiltrator. Screaming "God help me" with the shite literally running down my leg, I thought I needed a refuge. I wasn't going back to Betty's, as they would be waiting for me there for sure! I thought I'd look for a police station and state my case, but no, they'd be looking for me too! (By now some of the people I had previously spoken to would have informed them.) So what could I do? I know—KILL MYSELF! Yes, that's the answer, I felt. They were going to kill me anyway. I thought again. No, the love of my family prevented this, and I thought, I still have a few minutes left. I panicked: "What the fuck can I do!" I screamed.

Looking out the window, I saw the sign for Cliffoney, Co. Sligo, as if things weren't bad enough! I knew this was very near the spot were old Mountbatten was blown up. That's it! I'll *have* to kill myself now—they'll be thinking I've returned to the scene of the crime! What a fuckin' mind-constructed dilemma! Okay, my last chance, the Catholic Church! I kept driving, and finally got to an ecclesiastical building. I didn't know if it were church or chapel! I didn't care—it was a sanctuary, as I saw it.

I kicked on the big barn doors with all my might, shouting, "Help, help! They're going to kill me!"

Creak, creak, and the door was ajar. An old clergyman said, "For fuck sake, son, what's the problem?"

Yes, he swore! He was only human, after all.

"What's the problem!" I gasped. "They're going to kill me, is all! They're going to kill me!"

"Who?" he said.

"The Provos! The UDA! The police! They think I killed Mountbatten! They think I'm a Provo, they think I'm in the IRA!"

What the fuck was the old man to think? What *was* I, an IRA, a UDA member that killed Lord Mountbatten? Keep dreaming, Paul!

"You'll have to take me in!" I pleaded.

I had no more chance of a snowball's chance in hell.

"On your way, my son," the reverential gentleman said, "on your way!"

I thought, typical Catholic Church! As I now knew from the old bastard's dog collar, if I had given him money he would probably have given me a night's sanctuary, at least!

So away I went with minutes to suicide, but the love for my family kicked in again. "Just fight the wankers, Paul," I told myself. "But you'll need a gun!" came the rational thought in reply. Where the fuck was I to get a gun? Did the Garda carry guns? "I'll just look for one, and run him or her over," came another rational thought. But it was a tall order to take on the whole IRA, UDA and the Irish police force with one dead Garda's gun, in my paranoid state. I thought of the saying, "You can get anything at all in the AA, except alcohol," and knowing this to be true I thought I'd get a gun there off some cunt—there's all sorts in AA meetings, but then (another rational thought)—why would they get me a gun? They are full of love. Well, most are, I guess.

I got to a meeting and ran in like a man possessed.

"I'm Paul and I'm an alcoholic!" I shouted, "Get me a gun, get me a gun!"

When I think about it now, I could curl up and die. But there are crazier people than me in AA, though don't be put off by this admission: it's the greatest organisation in the world, bringing peace to millions!

The chairperson told me to be quiet as he wanted, quite rightly, to proceed with the meeting. The members just took it in their stride as they had seen it all before—people disrupting meetings, although perhaps not to this degree.

"Fuck you's," I said, "time is of the essence! I'll just go and hand myself in to the cop shop, at least they'll not shoot me. They might torture me though." Those were my thoughts. At least I would still be living and protected from the paramilitaries. So I jumped into the still running jeep and looked for the nearest police station.

There it was! Just round the corner, thank fuck! Relief beyond relief!

"Listen!" I shouted to the nice young policeman at the front desk, "I'm not a Provo or a UDA member, and I certainly didn't kill Louis Mountbatten, but I need you to arrest me, and if you don't I'm going to smash my jeep through your front window! I'm a sober alkie and I need help!"

"Sober alkie?" he must have thought, "what the fuck's that?" It's just the same as a clean junkie, or a non-performing sex addict, or a non-gambling gambler, but back to my calamity. He said, "On your way, ya silly drunk Scots bastard!"

I hadn't had a drink for ten months, but I was staying put! I threw myself on the hard tiled floor and shouted, "I'm fucking going nowhere!"

Out came a Garda officer, who I can only describe as gargantuan. He grabbed me like a rag doll, and I'm big! He threw me onto the street. I thought, "Tattie-pickin' Fenian bastard, my life's at risk here, ya fukin' ejit!"

That was it! I jumped in the jeep and drove it through the large panoramic window. They'll jail me *now*, I thought, and probably wouldn't see the jeep again.

They rushed out like the Charge of the Light Brigade. I was laughing, knowing that the Provos and the UDA wouldn't get me now! I was a certainty for the jail! With batons drawn, six of them ushered me horizontally to what I thought was the torture chamber, but torture was better than death.

"What the fuck's up with you, jock? Get your hands on your head!"

I duly accommodated them, hand on the napper. I shouted, "I'm innocent, I'm innocent!"

"Innocent of *what*?"

"Smashing the jeep through your window!" I said, "Guilty as charged!" was my cry, and added: "But I didn't kill Louie and I'm not a paramilitary!" Here we go again and the band played on.

"You're a nut case," said the big giant bobby.

"I want a lawyer," I said. "I'm a member of AA, and yes you can get anything you like in AA!"

One of the baton-holding policemen said, "Are you a friend of Doctor Bobs?"

I thought, "Nirvana, that's one of our world wide codes meaning a nice way of asking you if you're an alkie." I'm not at liberty to reveal any of the hundreds of codes, but I knew the officer had an insight into the fellowship. "Yes," I said.

He told the other officers to leave and began talking to me in a civilised manner. "What's your name?" he asked.

"I'm Paul and I'm an alcoholic," I said.

"Nice to meet you," he said. "My name is Liam. What's the story, Paul?"

I told him my tale of woe, and he immediately asked my home telephone number. I duly informed him. He proceeded to phone my mother and I could hear the two-way conversation.

"Hello, is this Paul's mother?" he said.

"Paul who…"

He turned to me. "Paul, what's your second name?"

"McGoldrick," I told him.

"Mrs McGoldrick," he said, back on the phone, "this is Sligo police. We have your son in custody."

"What's wrong?" said Anna. "He does have mental health problems," she elucidated.

"That's it?" He looked relieved. "Don't worry, Mrs McGoldrick, he's in safe hands. We'll be in touch."

Down went the phone. Liam gave me a big cuddle and said, "Don't worry, Paul. I know the crack."

I've got tears in my eyes as I write this. "I'm bi-polar, Paul," he smiled.

Why is he not wearing glasses, I thought. I still thought of my illness, then, as manic depression, even though I doubted it very much; then realised I was thinking of bi-focal! I'm thick as dung, ha ha!

He suggested I go down the local nutcracker suite and talk with the shrinks. This was—and I can't believe it!—to be on a voluntary basis, after all the carnage of the window smashing, etc. I thought I would have been sectioned this time I went like a dog out of trap five. I'd be among nice people, and the paramilitaries might not get me there! A huge wave of relief came over me and my paranoia was gone, in a flash.

They rang up the hospital and down I went to the loony-bin. I went with Liam to his Malachy College, and he told me he suffered a lot of suicidal depression. I was admitted with the best of courtesy, shown to my beautiful room and put on constant observation, for the fear of doing anything harmful to myself.

This is where I met Sinaed, a wee Irish colleen with a heart of gold, a staff nurse by trade, who had an answer for all my questions no matter what the subject. My paranoia had gone, as I said earlier, but I still had rapid speech until the sleepers kicked in. I was never as glad to take meds in all my life.

Chapter Nine

TWO WEEKS PASSED and off I went again, my sister Betty picking me up with her beautiful kids, and heading for her home. En route I stopped for the Irish *Autotrader*, as I needed wheels to continue my world tour, which was to take me to England, France, Spain, Tenerife, Turkey and Florida.

I bought the first vehicle I telephoned for, having the audacity of asking the vendor to drive it to me for a viewing, assuring him if it was what he said it was I would buy it. True to his word, there it was—a five-year-old Mitsubishi Shogun, shining like a new shilling on Oprah Winfrey's forearm. The deal done, I said goodbye to Bet, Paul and the kids, assuring them I was fine, fine, being FUCKED UP, INSECURE, NEUROTIC AND EMPTY, as the saying goes.

Nevertheless, I was paranoid-free and felt I was in heaven, yet again despatching the meds in the nearest bin. Some scrounging junkie could have had a field day—there was enough there to kill 50 buffalos!

I headed over the border into Ballyshanon and filled up with cheaper diesel. All along the road there were droves of people hitchhiking, girls alone even, plus many groups of many nationalities. I would never have done this in Britain, but I pulled over to a bunch of ladies my own age and asked them where they were going.

"Dublin, Scotchy," they replied.

"Ah fuck it, I'm going to Dublin also," I said, "jump in!"—and in they got, Brigitte, Siobhan, Kerry and Carmel. What a craic! They made Chubby Brown and Billy Connolly look like the Pope!

"Paul," one said, "git yir balls out fur the girls! We've heard you're hung like a horse!"

Not a drink between them as well!

"Paul," said Tara, "I'm a hooker in Limerick. A guy came in one night and said, 'How much is it for a wank?' I said £15 and the guy said, 'How much is it if you're not a wank?'"

This was the banter all the way. I told them some of my scary paramilitary story, and they said I was a brave man. I shared my story of the loony bins, and they took it with a pinch of salt! Not wanting to get out the jeep in Dublin without taking me for dinner, they suggested a local Chinese, so off we went. Chicken *ding* was the order all round—that's chicken in the microwave! We had a howl and filled our bellies with exotic side dishes all night. We all hugged and kissed, exchanged telephone numbers, email, and went on our ways. I find the Irish, both sides, the best in the world for not being judged mental, may your own God bless you all.

When I got back to my jeep the locks had been picked. All my belongings were gone! It wasn't much, but I had a couple of sentimental photos which I miss. The bastards had the cheek to leave me my prized possession of £1 PLASTIC ROSARIY BEADS which I got at knock the previous day. I've mentioned I'm not religious, but I'll go into a synagogue, a church, chapel or mosque and enjoy the tranquillity; but I bought these beads for Gran and Granda's grave; being plastic they wouldn't perish—a good deal for a pound. No, I'm just a miserable bar steward.

I booked into a local hostel, stayed up all night writing my memoirs, had breakfast and headed for my next casualties. This is when I met Kay, from the North Island of New Zealand, a real diamond. She was hitching on her own in Dublin, a brave girl! It was throwing it down, as if all the angels in heaven were incontinent. She had a big Berghaus jacket fully zipped and hooded on her beautiful frame. I pulled over thinking it was a guy! I was shocked to find out she was of the female persuasion when she said good morning and asked where I was going. Where was she heading, I asked? She said Belfast in a smashing Kiwi accent, and I thought, well, I'm going to Belfast too! I would have gone to Timbuktu with this beauty and paid the spaceship flight tickets as well.

"Hop in!" I said.

"Thanks," she replied, and I was in double heaven.

First things first, I thought, let's call into Betty's on the road back, to reassure Kay I was not some kind of mass murderer who picked up lone females on a dull city road. She said, "Don't worry, we'll be fine."

I thought, what! She wants to marry me? Or was it the jeep? Does she want a free meal ticket? To the unsuspecting public the jeep looked, maybe, 40 or 50 grand! We drove the few hours to Betty's and all was well.

Betty gave us dinner and listened to my tales of new-found fortune. Kay and I decided to tour Ireland and set out for the Giant's Causeway. I think Betty thought, "Nothing surprises me with our Paul! Just met this bird, and decides to travel an island with her!" But I was fast, you see! When I was a kid I used to hit the light switch and say my prayers under the covers before the light was out.

Kay and I were fortunate enough to see the whole of Ireland, doing Belfast, Cork and Donegal, to mention a few. By this time Kay and I were in love! A month had passed and we had the most beautiful time on earth.

She decided to come home to Coatbridge with me and so she did—but it wasn't to last as most of my relationships took a slide due to my depression. All the girls stood by me in my times of despair, but I would either leave or ask them to go. I have been with over 200 girls in my life and I don't say that boastfully—there was very little penetrative sex, as I was always too drunk to funk, or I was impotent due to being bi-polar. God bless Viagra!

My current girlfriend, Mary, is a psychiatric nurse, would you believe it? Yes, a shrink's assistant! She has made it clear to me she is not my nurse, and I made it clear to her I will not be her patient.

Chapter Ten

IN AUGUST '98 I enrolled in college for an HNC in Healthcare, as I thought I had a wonderful insight into my illness. Like hell I did! My objective was to become a physic nurse, and I was given a placement in ward 24 and ward 25 at Monklands District General Hospital, psychiatric wing. There was me in my whites, proud as punch with my name badge firmly pinned on my chest—I had arrived! To hell with Freud and Karl Jung, bring on top psychotherapist and psychoanalyst Professor Paul McGoldrick—I was going to cure the world of mental illness.

I was later to become a resident of this fabulous hospital, for my head cracked again! I had more cracks than Humpty Dumpty, come to think of it. But whilst I was there I learned an awful lot. As I have already mentioned, I might have been mad, but I wasn't stupid! I have a mine of knowledge on mental health issues, but I can only explain them in layman's terms… But I'll not bore you with my layman's jargon—talk to the professionals!

I also have a vast knowledge as a sufferer and hope I'm letting you into a little insight in this book. Don't hesitate if you want a chat—my contact details are at the back of this book! Many thanks—united we stand, divided we fall! You are no longer alone: a problem shared is a problem halved.

Yes, my black cloud kicked in again and I was forced to drop out of college—but I'm very grateful for the short time I had, and will never forget it. If only I had taken my meds back at Stratheden in '97, who knows where I would be! But I'm not going to shut the door on the past—as I see it, it was my greatest asset. Yes Gran, I have learned by my mistakes, and I've a lot of damage to do yet—ha, ha! On a serious note, though, I try to love my neighbour as myself today, and try not to do anyone any harm. I did enough of that for 44 years! As I've said, I was a thief, a liar and a cheat—but I don't mean in the way you might imagine! Yes, I stole from my mum as a kid, but what nearly killed me was when it came home to me that in effect I had been stealing from the family income in more recent years. It's like the bible story of the widow's mite. I wasn't putting enough into the domestic coffers, you see. Take the person who is earning £100 pounds, for example, and puts the lot in—he is putting in more than the guy who is earning, say, £300, and puts in only half. That was me—so yes, I was a thief by not declaring my means. And I told more lies than Tam Pepper to cover this up! So there you have it—a thief, liar 'n cheat!

Thankfully it's not like that today. I put three quarters in. It is in giving that we receive—how profound is that! I believe the best thing we can give anyone is our time. Basically, it's all we have. Let's face it, whatever we've got in this world, we've only got on loan. For each one of us it will all be taken away at one time, for sadly each one of us will die one day; but as far as I'm concerned, there is no need to be anxious about this. But I'm not ready for the big house in the sky just yet!

I love the story of St. Augustine, the great womaniser, who, when he had the final call from his God, wanted a little extra time. It goes like this. The big yin said to him, "Augustine, come, come, my son!" But at that particular time he was with a gorgeous woman, see, and so he replied, "Give me ten minutes, father." Saint Paul, the man who apparently slew lorry-loads of Christians, changed for the better, so I'm told, so why can't we?

I was once asked, "How many therapists does it take to change a light bulb? The correct answer? Just one, but the light bulb must *want* to change. I was also told that if I want to change the world I had to start with myself. I thought, what a load of shite! But I see it clearly today, and it's given me the most wonderful life: the best way to peace of mind is to mind my own business! That's what I incorporate these days. Now it's Monday morning, the 30th November 2009. Just now, as I write my scattered memoirs here at 00.53 a.m., I'm thinking of all the moral teachings of my parents and grandparents. It is not 2000 BC or earlier, and the same moral teachings still apply. But I keep it simple today and simply see it all as love—and I don't mean sex!

From the big hard nut I was as a youth, the IRA member in 1981, and as some would have said, the thief, the liar and the cheat—call me what you like—you don't know what you're missing if you don't really know me as I am today. My thing now is going out for meals, on a budget, may I add, sharing a bath with my girlfriend—the water can sometimes jump out, mind you—whilst we listen to the panpipes of South America! Can you hear them, or perhaps some classic classicals to accompany the candles, massage and aromatherapy? To that add a big bag of wine gums and six Mars Bars, and twenty-odd smuggled golden Virginia backy rollups—Nirvana! A recipe for a stroke or heart failure? You better believe it—but I just love it!

I believe what's meant for you won't go by you. As Gran said, when it's time to get off the bus, it's time to get off the bus! When your number's up, your number's up! Having said that, I'm 21-stone today and I can still do 3.3 minutes on the bags at Rab Bannen's barn boxing gym, and I smoke in excess of 70 rollups a day. So whoever or whatever it is, I know someone or something is looking after me. Like most of us, I think at some time we've all been to hell and back, or hell will come like the grim reaper some day—so please, please keep your faith!

KNOW GOD, NO FEAR—KNOW FEAR, NO GOD! This has been a wonderful statement for me, and whoever your God is, remember there is only One. I was told that if you struggle with God, add another 'o', and that makes it good! Yes, I tried the power of good and believe me, it works—in my thoughts and in my words and deeds.

But old habits die hard. I'm not ready to be elected the new Dalai Lama just yet. Today I pray for nothing but God's will for me—that and nothing else, but prayers of thanks. I don't know who or what I'm praying to, but billions can't be wrong.

Recently my sister Katrina was diagnosed with breast cancer and went on to have her breast removed. Now the old me would have been the drama queen I was, and looked for a drink to drown my selfish sorrows. But I handed it over quite simply to my higher power, asking only for the knowledge of his will for me, and the power to carry it out. Part of the 12-step recovery programme in AA, you see, and what came back to me was just to be there for her and give her my support. So Katrina, who I love dearly in the old McGoldrick fashion, came home from Torquay in Devon to have a cancer party, her final celebration.

Did I say final celebration! Not a bit of it! It's five years down the line and she's cured, happy as a pig in shite, so yet again I state my case—it's not over till the fat lady sings!

Chapter Eleven

BACK TO THE HOLY BOOKS! In my opinion, words like *holy* simply mean, whole, together, etc. This leads me to the interpretation of *sane*, mentioned many times in the holy books of Islam, Judaism, Christianity, etc. In my research I was to find out that down the ages, from Sanskrit to Hebrew and Latin, that *sane* means only one thing and one thing only—PERFECT. So in my humble opinion anyone who is saying they are sane are saying they are perfect—and therefore saying they are the god of their own understanding! I rest my case, my learned friends. I choose to stay that little bit insane today, as we need it to go through this crazy life (which suffers from an excess of sanity). Well, I do anyway—what about you?

On a funny note: I used to go to Nunraw Abbey, a working Trappist monastery near Haddington in Edinburgh, and one day I had a chat with one of the Fathers. I said, "Father, I'm not going back to chapel." In his cool way he asked, "Why not, Paul?" I said, "It's full of hypocrites!" I got my answer. Quite calmly, and without delay, he said, "There's room for one more, Paul."

I don't know if you find that funny, as you can kid with some of the people some of the time, but you can't kid with all of the people all of the time. But that's what I thought! You see, I was so screwed up I thought I'd go up and give these monks some of my wisdom and see if they could cure me! Since then I have had the pleasure of visiting Pluscarten Abbey in Elgin, Morayshire, in Scotland, as well as Rossnowlagh near Ballyshanon, and met many protestant friends in all these places. I also go to protestant churches on a regular basis which I thoroughly enjoy, especially in Florida: the patter is magic and the message is all the same wherever I go—church, chapel, synagogue or mosque: LOVE THY NEIGHBOUR AS THYSELF, DO UNTO OTHERS WHAT YOU WOULD HAVE DONE UNTO YOU. SO BE IT! Thanks mum, you were right again, and to my old crabit bugger of a father, thanks for the advice of YOUR FAVOURITE SAYING: DON'T HOLD GRUDGES, LIFE'S TOO SHORT!

Today when I see or phone my family and friends, male or female, I tell them I love them as I leave or hang up, for who knows, it might be the last time I see or hear from them. To Peter who robbed me of £600 whilst I was in early recovery in AA, and James who stole my car, Patricia, who robbed me of £3,500, and all the rest who took advantage of my mental illness, well, you are all forgiven. If you so desire, put all of the money or part of it into a charity of your choice. LIFE'S TOO SHORT! After all, I did my fair share of wrong in my life, and yes, I'm not a Buddhist or anything, but I do believe in karma, simplified to what goes around comes around.

Call me what you may, but I don't believe there's any bad in the world. I believe there is plenty of wrong, and wrongs can always be corrected—a powerful statement, I know, but I've got to speak my truth. It will set me free, and it has!

I'm sitting here thinking of St. Andrew, the patron saint of Scotland. God bless him as I'm finally proud of my Scots heritage. I always claimed to be Irish, even regularly speaking in an Irish accent. Whay a lot of bullshit, I thinks now! And for what I don't know. Yes, I was just a Walter Mitty for many a year, and a mad one at that!

Chapter Twelve

NOW I'LL DESCEND INTO MY SHENANIGANS in Istanbul. If you hear me out, I'll be much obliged!

In August 2000 I decided I was off to Turkey to sort out the world's heroin problem. Who did I think I was—a one man CIA or FBI? Well, why not, because I was... yes, you guessed it, manic once more!

I landed in the picturesque village of Bodrum on the south west coast, all alone as usual, and immediately set up my own business as auctioneer to the highest shop owner bidder. They were amazed, to say the least!

The plan was that I would go on the mike and sell their goods—yes, their whole shop within two hours, moving hundreds of real fake clothes! The pitch went something like this: "CURENTLY SELLING IN ALL YOUR TOP DEPARTMENT STORES AT 9.99" (Or whatever price was comparable). I went on: "NOW I MUST EMPHASIZE, WE DON'T SELL CHEAP QUALITY GOODS! WHAT WE DO IS SELL TOP QUALITY GOODS CHEAP!" This was the one that got the British tourists' attention. I added in a few of my previous school lines: "NO FANCY SHOPS AND NO

FANCY PRICES!" And the shops were jumping! I would record my voice onto an old tape recorder and let it blare out when I wanted a rest. Out went the merchandise, Levi, Armani, Hugo, Boss, Adidas, the works! The Turks thought I was some kind of messiah, and the Brits and Irish had a bargain. I made an awful lot of money, certainly more than one man could use in a few months. I had agreed a commission deal with the owners when I initially met them to discuss the deals.

But low and behold, I was driven out of town with the Kurdish mafia, gun at head, once again, as some shop owners became very jealous of their competitors' new-found success. Funnily enough I found out it was the traders whom I had previously asked if they wanted the deal that paid the mafia. Who's sorry now, was all I could think.

So with a big bag of money in tail, I jumped on the dolomush, took it to the bus station, and jumped on a bus for anywhere, destination unknown. After a while I saw signs for Marmaris. A few minutes passed and we drew up at Marmaris bus station, to start the same proceedings again. Nine times out of ten, when you're manic, nothing scares you. So out came the shooters again and I was off to Kusadasi this time. Yes, blah blah blah, history repeated itself and I was off to Istanbul.

Three months had passed and I was a wealthy manic man, with a five-figure sum tucked down my balls 'n pockets 'n sleeves 'n socks—the lot, and I mean lira, so you can imagine the bulk! I was a multi-multi lira millionaire, worth a robbing. Yes, and that was what was to materialise. Like the dickhead I was, flashing money in all of the cafes, Burger Kings and McDonalds, I left one night to go home to my Turkish abode and was held up by five Africans, and all I could think of was, "I kept you bastards when I was at primary school!" I reached out and struck a blow at the gunman but missed, and they knocked me to the ground, rifling all my pockets etc.

So there I was, destitute and homeless, for if I didn't get my rent, I had nowhere to live. I went straight back to my microphone commodities. The money wasn't as good, but enough to get by. I felt like a destitute prostitute who was looking for an institute. I took jobs as a bouncer on the door of the Rhythm Bar in Taxim where the Leeds United incident happened, and my my, were the Asian birds good in bed! I was back in heaven!

Memet, whom I got to know really well, was the local PR for one of the back street brothels, and for weeks he pressurised me with his persuasive banter to come down and be part of the scene there. I would tell him to go and fuck himself! I had a great relationship with him and could talk to him in this manner, no problem—after all, why would I want to go to a whorehouse when I was shagging a different Naomi Campbell every night? The Viagra was on tap everywhere you went in Istanbul, the counterfeit capital of the world at that time, or so I was led to believe. Memet, I thought, was a sound guy—and because he said I would only have to buy one coffee, I went down on the understanding that *he* would pick up the tab. I could imagine the price of the coffee! Again, mad but not stupid, see? You could probably buy all the coffee in South America for the price in a Turkish whorehouse! I had dealings with them before—not the whorehouses, the Turks and their coffee, and yes, unusually for me, I was bang on correct!

We proceeded to go down a few dark narrow lanes. Up ahead in the distance I saw a glimmering light. Does that ring a bell? It could be a portal to heaven or a portal to hell! In we went, met by a couple of big ugly 25-stone Turkish gorillas, and Memet said, "*E ak sham lar,*" shook their shovels, and proceeded to the main gallery. He said tea or coffee, or something stronger, or maybe coke or orange juice. I said coffee as I knew he had agreed to take the bill!

Over came King Kong and Godzilla and roared in broken English: "You want to meet the ladies!" "Chase yir sell lads," I said, as if they knew what that meant, and they said, "Wot you say Jeemy?" meaning Jimmy. I take it Memet told them I was Scottish.

"Go fuk yirsel," was my response, and they went ballistic: "You bastard! You bastard! You…"

"Hurry, shoot me, shoot me!" I laughed at them.

"Not say fuk! You not say fuk! We kill you! We kill you!" they ranted.

"Kill me then," I grinned, "you black enamel bastard!"

Memet was off like a bullet from a pumped up Armalite. Out came the star pistol that I recognised from my previous escapades and enquiries at the Irish bar just up the road.

"What you waiting on?" I taunted. "Better weather?"

One of them hit me with a slap that would have knocked out a rhino. In this case, thank heavens for mania, as it makes you super strong. Over came the manager, a puny little ethnic man who could speak perfect English, who asked what the problem was. I explained the situation and he shrugged his shoulders and suggested I paid for the coffee—one cup—and he said "That will be 50 million lira." In those days I think it was a pound to the lira or thereabouts—in other words, fifty quid for a coffee!

I gave him much the same reply I had already given to the gorillas.

"You wanker, you wanker, where's your money?" he screamed at me, clearly having lost his cool.

"Your brothers robbed me of it a few nights ago," I said urbanely. "Now you're getting fuck all."

"I'll shoot you! I'll shoot you!" He was becoming quite hysterical at this point.

"Well, fukin' shoot me then, ya wanker," I said, knowing he knew what a wanker was.

"MONEY, MONEY!" he screamed.

I thought on my feet. Now I knew they were Kurdish, not Turkish, for obvious reasons. I knew they would know of the PKK, known as Kurdish Freedom Fighters to some—so I knew they would have heard of the IRA. This was my thinking at the time, and it worked a treat! Brothers in arms, as all I could think of was another Naomi waiting on my Greek Adonis body up at the Rhythm Bar. I said calmly, "I'm patron of the IRA bar further up the road, so shoot me if you dare."

They looked at me nonplussed.

"Bang bang bang bang bang!" I said calmly again.

Now 'patron' in Turkey means owner, so what did they think? I think they concluded I was a wealthy man, i.e. a man of power, and that I had an IRA connection, therefore one to be feared. I was so convincing, if I say so myself!

NOT A BAD BIT OF INTELLIGENCE FOR A MAD MAN, what! When I say 'mad' I don't mean 'bad'. Typical bullies—stand up to them, I say, and they (the bullies) will run a mile!

Back to mad and not bad. I have been called Big Mad McGoldrick recently by a few friends, and honestly, it doesn't bother me at all. I love them dearly, and I must expect this for the rest of my life! Unless I do a Lord Lucan, no thanks—I'm here to stay, like it or lump it! You see, I name-called for years before my diagnosis. This was because I was a sick, sick, cookie, not happy with self, always willing to condemn others, as it was easier than looking at my own mountain of character defects, for didn't I tell you I was riddled with the seven deadly sins? I only hope and pray that others don't have to go through what I had to.

Love, peace and best wishes to the world!

Yours,

Big Mad McGoldrick

To be continued…

P.S. Remember, sane means perfect…

Paul McGoldrick can be contacted on:

Email: paulliam6@hotmail.com
Tel number: 00 44 (0) 7518 832426

BRASS KERB

Lightning Source UK Ltd
Milton Keynes UK
15 October 2010

161335UK00001B/2/P